Grade 1

Improve your piano grade 1!

Paul Harris & Richard Crozier

FABER *ff* MUSIC

The syllabus referenced in this anthology is © Copyright by The Associated Board of the Royal Schools of Music and is reproduced by permission of the copyright owner.

© 2014 by Faber Music Ltd
This edition first published in 2014
Bloomsbury House 74–77 Great Russell Street London WC1B 3DA
Music processed by MacMusic
Cover and text designed by Susan Clarke
Printed in England by Caligraving Ltd
All rights reserved

ISBN10: 0-571-53881-9
EAN13: 978-0-571-53881-2

To buy Faber Music publications or to find out about the full range of titles available please contact your local music retailer or Faber Music sales enquiries:
Faber Music Ltd, Burnt Mill, Elizabeth Way, Harlow CM20 2HX
Tel: +44 (0) 1279 82 89 82 Fax: +44 (0) 1279 82 89 83
sales@fabermusic.com fabermusicstore.com

Contents

Introduction

This book outlines an interactive, collaborative and imaginative way to teach pieces that have been set for an exam syllabus. The whole philosophy of teaching the Simultaneous Learning way is that we are pro-active rather than reactive. We take the ingredients of a piece and explore them in imaginative ways, making connections between them, being creative and enabling pupils to learn in a really engaging way. Students should be encouraged to continue with these activities in their practice. Not only do they learn to play the piece, but they can then apply their understanding to learn further pieces more quickly. It is a positive and exciting process that supports thorough learning and the potential for greater progress and continuing achievement.

How to use this book

The work on each piece is divided into three periods:
1 Preliminary work before you introduce the notation;
2 Work when you are learning the piece from the notation and
3 Refining the piece ready for performance.

The amount of time spent on each period will depend on how students respond to the activities and how quickly they absorb the ingredients and concepts. Many instructions (describe, discuss, identify, explore, etc.) are intended to be carried out collaboratively with the student.

One of the important reasons for adopting Simultaneous Learning is to get away from the 'beginning at bar one and correcting mistakes as they are inevitably made' approach. Instead, we identify the ingredients of each piece, discuss and explore them through imaginative and appropriate activities and by making up (improvising) very simple musical ideas. Through experimentation and mixing and matching the ingredients, pupils will ultimately learn the pieces in a much more secure and musical way, at the same time deepening their general musical understanding.

Getting started

Play the piece yourself and note the ingredients (they are also listed on each worksheet). Think about the music in terms of each individual student's particular needs and abilities. Look at the suggested activities and decide which ones are most appropriate for the student in that particular lesson, and which order you might like to introduce them. There is no set way to do this – you can begin with whichever you think is best. In the Simultaneous Learning way, if each activity is carefully chosen and each subsequent activity is carefully related and/or sequential, then your student should always achieve. Progress will be natural and ongoing. Do remember that in the first lesson on any new piece (and perhaps for several more lessons, too) the book is better closed and out of sight; try to rely more on your ear, memory and imagination.

Once you start these activities many more will become apparent – simply go with what works and your intuition. Begin anywhere appropriate in each piece – only occasionally at bar 1! Don't always start with the right hand but encourage students to experiment with playing right-hand patterns in the left hand and vice versa. If you have other ideas, do bring them into your teaching: let your imagination take flight! As students gain in confidence, awareness and understanding you can connect these activities with new ones. The dotted lines on each page direct us to the kind of connections we can make as our lessons unfold, and they remind us that all areas of music are linked.

There is no precise amount of time to spend on any particular set of activities and no set order. As you get used to teaching in this way the timing will become second nature. Start by aiming to spend about a third of the lesson on the activities set out on each page (but if you spend an entire lesson on these activities it is time well spent). If the student finds them straightforward then move on – either developing them further or moving on to new ones.

Improvisation is suggested regularly in this book. This doesn't mean jazz improvisation or making up entire pieces. It's about creating little musical fragments, phrases, patterns or exercises using ingredients from the piece. Begin with just one or two notes and move on from there – it's really very simple. Students love this and it brings their learning and understanding of the key elements of a piece to life in a vivid and meaningful way. Develop the habit of improvising regularly – you'll find it a huge help in your teaching.

Call and response is clapping or playing a short phrase to the student, who responds by clapping or playing it back. It's useful for helping students become familiar with new rhythms, dynamics, articulations and so on. **Question and answer** is a little more sophisticated – a short phrase is answered by something slightly different, which complements the musical question. It could be an altered note or rhythm, or a change to the dynamic or articulation. Both are simple, enjoyable and creative activities that develop understanding in a musical way.

For students using this book (with or without a teacher)

This may be the first time you have used the Simultaneous Learning approach. Rather than simply 'playing through the piece', using these activities will encourage you to explore and experiment and really get to know the music thoroughly. The advantage of working this way is that you should find it much easier to apply the principles from one piece to another. Time spent 'off the piece', working with its ingredients, should prove much more valuable than simply playing straight through. Learning by copying your teacher may have its place, but it is a short-term strategy and will not ultimately help you to develop and become a confident, independent musician.

The Simultaneous Learning map

The Simultaneous Learning Map is a graphic representation of what we as musicians and teachers instinctively know. The map depicts the various areas of music and the fact that they all connect. This representation is not entirely accurate as of course all the areas connect. Most teachers and pupils will wish the teaching to be based around a piece or song, so that is placed in the centre. Just how we move around the map will be determined by a combination of teacher experience, how the pupil is responding and how the lesson is unfolding. The beauty of Simultaneous Learning and its map is that there are infinite possibilities. Teachers can make the process their own.

For more detail on this see *Simultaneous Learning: The definitive guide* (Faber Music).

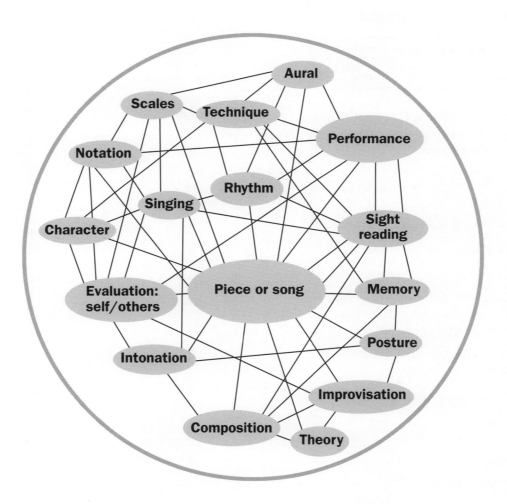

Arietta (Clementi)

All about... grace, elegance and delicacy

Pre-notation activities

Rhythm

- Clap a suitable pulse in $\frac{2}{4}$.
- Play call-and-response clapping games using two-bar phrases from *Arietta*:

- Move on to longer phrases:

- If there is space, repeat these while walking round the room to the pulse.

Dynamics

- Play a C major one-octave scale and broken chord:
  - *p* and then *f*
  - with a *crescendo* ascending and *diminuendo* descending
- Play call-and-response games using short phrases in C major in $\frac{2}{4}$ that explore these dynamics.

Aural

- Listen to a performance of *Arietta*.
- Clap the pulse as you listen to the performance, emphasising the strong beat of the bar.
- Describe the articulation and dynamics in this piece.

Improvisation

- Improvise some music in C major and $\frac{2}{4}$ using light articulation and two- and four-note slurs. Include triad shapes and add dynamics.

Key and scale patterns

- Play the scale and broken chord of C major in each hand from memory and notation.
- Play the scale (or part of the scale) using this rhythm on each note:

Title, character and context

- Find out what the title *Arietta* means.
- Listen to any other pieces called *Arietta* that you can find.

Introducing the notation (opening the book)

Rhythm

- Find any recurring rhythmic patterns in the piece.
- Tap out these rhythms from the notation. Continue until the rhythm of both hands can be tapped fluently.
- Try tapping the rhythm of both hands together, section by section. Make sure the rests are clear.

Pulse

- Set up a $\frac{2}{4}$ pulse. Play two bars (hands separately or together), then count (aloud or silently) and hear the two bars internally. Play the next two bars and so on.

Aural

- Talk about whether the piece is major or minor and describe the dynamics.
- Sing back some two-bar phrases from *Arietta* (probably down an octave).
- Play a phrase from the piece twice. The second time make a change for the student to identify.

Dynamics

- Circle all the dynamics in the music with different colours for the different levels.
- Explore the *crescendo* and *diminuendo* shapes (this will eventually help with the phrasing).
- Look at these in the music and discuss where more might be added.

Key and scale patterns*

- Discuss the key of the piece.
- Find patterns based on the scale and broken chord of C major in *Arietta*.
- Discuss triad patterns and find any in the piece.
- Learn left-hand bars 8–12 from memory, noticing the pattern. Make up a right-hand tune above it.

Title, character and context

- Discuss the title.
- Think of some words to describe the character of the music. Make up some music in C major based around this character.
- Find out some facts about Clementi.

* For more help with scales and broken chords, try the C major Finger Fitness section in *Improve your scales!* Grade 1.

Playing and refining the piece

Rhythm and pulse

- Check the rhythms are all understood.
- Make up some music to explore the rhythms in *Arietta*.
- Try the piece as a clapping duet, one person clapping each hand.
- Try playing the piece at different speeds.

Key and scale patterns

- Regularly play the scale and broken chord of C major and A minor in an elegant and *Arietta*-like style.
- Discuss the connection between these keys.
- Sight-read a piece in C major.*

Aural

- Regularly try to hear the piece internally – just the rhythm at first, then the melody too.
- Visualise your hands at the keyboard playing the piece at the same time as hearing it internally.
- Describe the dynamic shape of *Arietta*.

Balance and dynamics

- Take four-bar phrases from *Arietta* and work on the dynamics (especially *cresc.* and *dim.*) and the balance between the hands.
- Sing the phrases then try playing them with the same phrasing.

Title, character and context

- Think about the character – does it suggest a picture, story or mood?
- Make up some words to fit the melody of *Arietta*.
- Listen to some more piano pieces by Clementi.

Performing

- Start performing the piece all the way through, hands separately as well as together.
- Make sure there is a sense of phrasing and that the rests are clear.
- Perform the whole piece to relatives and friends and/or make a recording.

* For suitable sight-reading pieces try *Improve Your Sight-reading!* Grade 1.

Student's worksheet

Arietta ingredients

Key signature C major
Time signature 2/4
Rhythms

Dynamics *p f* < >
Articulation Gently separated, slurs
Character Elegant and polite
Form A B A'

Terms and signs
Allegretto ♩ = c.100
Special ingredients
Rocking left hand and hand balance in bars 8–12

☐ Explore these ingredients by making up little musical patterns, exercises or phrases. Mix and match them where you can. Tick each ingredient when you've used it.

☐ Write out the last four bars of *Arietta*, both hands, complete with all signs and markings:

- Write the names under all the left-hand notes.
- Put a bracket above or below any semitones.
- What is the name of the highest right-hand note? _____
- What is the name and time value of the shortest note? _____
- Play the music from your own notation.

☐ Sight-read this piece and list the ingredients here:

Andante

☐ Write a two-bar rhythm as an answer to this rhythm, then clap it:

Minuet in G (Haydn)

All about... dance, four-bar phrases and a neat left hand

Pre-notation activities

Rhythm and pulse

- Clap a suitable pulse in $\frac{3}{4}$:
  - student claps all beats;
  - teacher claps a strong 1 and student weaker 2 & 3;
  - student claps a strong 1 and teacher 2 & 3.
- Talk about and explore these note values:

- Play call-and-response clapping games using two-bar phrases such as:

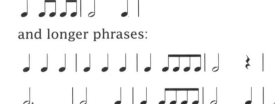

and longer phrases:

Dynamics

- Play a G major scale and broken chord:
  - *p*, *mf* and *f*
  - with a *crescendo* ascending and *diminuendo* descending.
- Play call and response using short phrases in $\frac{3}{4}$, exploring the dynamics in *Minuet in G*.

Special ingredients

- Explore octaves (bar 4, 7, 8, 15 and 16).
- Explore sevenths (left-hand bar 4, right-hand bars 9 and 12-13).
- Explore sixths (bar 3).

Aural

- Listen to a performance of *Minuet in G*. Notice the dynamics and articulation of the piece.
- Clap the pulse as you listen to the performance, emphasising the strong beat of the bar.

Title, character and context

- Listen to some minuets.
- Find out about the minuet dance and how the steps fit with the three beats in a bar.

Key and scale patterns

- Play the scale and broken chord of G major in each hand from memory and from notation.
- Play the scale (or part of the scale) using this rhythm on each note:

or

Introducing the notation (opening the book)

Rhythm

- Find any recurring rhythmic patterns, such as:

- Identify the upbeats within the piece.

- Clap the rhythms from the notation until secure. Continue until able to tap both hands separately and then (section by section) hands together.

- Work at any rhythms that are still uncertain.

Aural

- Discuss whether the piece is major or minor and describe the dynamics.

- Play a phrase from the piece twice. The second time make a change for the student to identify.

Pulse

- Set up a pulse. Play two bars (hands separately or together), then count and think the next two bars internally, then play the next two bars and so on.

- Notice how the left hand provides a continuous pulse in this piece (except in bar 11).

- Clap along with some other minuets, emphasising the 3-in-a-bar feel.

Key and scale patterns*

- Find any patterns in the piece based on the scale and broken chord of G major.

- Identify any accidentals and discuss which key they belong to.

- Explore the fingerings and hand position changes.

- Which left-hand bar contains all the notes of a D major triad?

Dynamics

- Circle all the dynamics using different colours for the different levels.

- Explore the various dynamic levels in the music and notice how they fit the phrases.

- Look for where more could be added (e.g. *cresc.* and *dim.* in bars 1–4).

- Apply the dynamic levels to scales, broken chords and patterns from the piece.

Title, character and context

- Think of some words to describe the character of this piece.

- Watch people dancing a minuet online.

- Find out what musical period this piece is from.

- Find out some facts about Haydn.

* For more help with scales and broken chords, try the G major Finger Fitness section in *Improve your scales!* Grade 1.

Playing and refining the piece

Rhythm and pulse

- Try playing the piece at different speeds.
- Tap the rhythm of the whole piece with both hands at the same time. Include the dynamics.

Scales and broken chords

- Regularly play the scales of G and D major and broken chord of G major in an elegant, minuet-like style.
- Discuss the connection between these keys.
- Sight-read a piece in G major.*

Aural

- Regularly try to hear the piece internally – just the rhythm at first, then the melody too.
- Visualise your hands at the keyboard playing the piece at the same time as hearing it internally.
- Talk about the articulation and describe the dynamics in *Minuet in G*.

Articulation and dynamics

- Play sections concentrating on the light articulation, balance between the hands and dynamics to give the piece its character.
- Play the piece with completely different articulation and dynamics; discuss how it sounds.
- Refine the hand position changes.

Title, character and context

- Think about the character of the whole piece – does it suggest a picture, story or mood?
- Find out about eighteenth-century costume then draw a picture of a minuet being danced.

Performing

- Start performing the piece all the way through, hands separately as well as together.
- Focus on a singing melody in the right hand with a supporting but slightly quieter left hand.
- Perform the whole piece to relatives and friends and/or make a recording.

* For suitable sight-reading pieces try *Improve Your Sight-reading!* Grade 1.

Student's worksheet

Minuet in G ingredients

Key signature G major

Time signature $\frac{3}{4}$

Rhythms

Dynamics *f mf p cresc.*

Articulation Gently
separated, slurs

Character Dance-like, elegant

Form Binary

Terms and signs
♩ = c.120, repeats and 1st
and 2nd time bars

Special ingredients
Octaves, sixths and
sevenths

☐ Explore these ingredients by making up little musical patterns, exercises or phrases.
Mix and match them where you can. Tick each ingredient when you've used it.

☐ Add the correct clef and any necessary sharps or flats to this G major scale.
Add a *crescendo* from *p* to *f*. Draw a bracket over the semitones.

☐ Sight-read this piece and list the ingredients here:

Moderato

☐ Write an explanation for what this means:

1.   2.

☐ Write out a two-bar rhythm from *Minuet in G* that appears at least four times in the piece:

$\frac{3}{4}$

☐ Find a picture of people dancing a minuet or draw your own.

The Lincolnshire Poacher (Trad. English)

All about... fun, lively rhythms and the end played as fast as possible!

Pre-notation activities

Rhythm

- Discuss $\frac{6}{8}$ then choose and clap a suitable pulse: one person claps dotted crotchets, the other claps quavers, then
  Skip to this rhythm.

- Discuss the upbeat and try some call and response using this phrase:

  Feel the pulse strongly.

- Play call-and-response clapping games using two-bar phrases:

  and then longer phrases of your choice.

Dynamics

- Play an F major scale and broken chord:
  - *p*, *mf* and *f*
  - with a *crescendo* ascending and *diminuendo* descending.

- Play call-and-response games using short phrases in $\frac{6}{8}$ exploring these dynamics.

Aural

- Listen to a performance of *The Lincolnshire Poacher*.

- Clap the pulse as you listen to the performance. Are there any changes of tempo?

Title, character and context

- Improvise some music in F major and $\frac{6}{8}$ using articulation and shapes from the piece.

- Find out what a poacher is and research other traditional songs from your country or region.

- Find Lincolnshire on a map of the UK.

Key and scale patterns

- Play the scale and broken chord of F major hands separately from memory and from notation.

- Play the scale (or part of the scale) using this rhythm on each note:

- Discuss the term 'chromatic'.

Introducing the notation (opening the book)

Rhythm

- Find any recurring rhythmic patterns and check if they are known well.
- How many times does the opening right-hand rhythm return?
- Try the piece as a clapping duet, one person clapping each hand.
- Discuss and explore tied notes. Clap the tied notes from the notation until secure.

Pulse

- Set up a pulse. Play two bars (hands separately or together), then count and hear the next two bars internally, then play the next two bars and so on.
- Clap along with other pieces in $\frac{6}{8}$, emphasising the two-in-a-bar feel.

Dynamics

- Circle all the dynamics using different colours for the different levels.
- Explore the various dynamic levels and notice how they fit the phrases. Look at these in the music and suggest any more markings that could be added.
- Apply these dynamics to scale and broken-chord patterns and patterns from the piece.

Key and scale patterns*

- Identify all the patterns in the piece that are based on the scale and broken chord of F major.
- Identify the small section of a chromatic scale in the piece.

Special ingredients

- Improvise some music with tempo changes. Then play bar 11 to the end.
- Explore chromatic shapes, looking specifically at bars 16–17.
- Improvise phrases in $\frac{6}{8}$ with pauses.
- Practise the left-hand chords in bars 9–13.

Title, character and context

- Listen to this song online and then sing it yourself.
- Make up a short story or cartoon to describe what you think is happening in the piece.
- Sing or play some other folk songs.

* For more help with scales and broken chords, try the F major Finger Fitness section in *Improve your scales!* Grade 1.

Playing and refining the piece

Rhythm and pulse

- Try playing the piece at different speeds.
- Tap the rhythm of the whole piece with both hands at the same time.

Scales and broken chords

- Play the scale and broken chord of F major and D minor with a bold, confident and rustic tone.
- Discuss the connection between these keys.
- Sight-read a piece in F major.*

Aural

- Regularly try to hear the piece internally – just the rhythm at first, then the melody too.
- Visualise your hands at the keyboard playing the piece at the same time as hearing it internally.
- Talk about the dynamics and changes of tempo in *The Lincolnshire Poacher*.
- Sing *The Lincolnshire Poacher*.

Articulation and dynamics

- Play sections completely *legato*, then with detached, slightly accented articulation.
- Try playing the piece with completely different dynamics, then play it with the given dynamics. How different does it sound?

Title, character and context

- Read the lyrics then draw a picture of or write a description of the Lincolnshire poacher.
- Write a story to fit the piece (including the pauses) and think about the meaning as you perform the piece.

Performing

- Start performing the piece all the way through, hands separately as well as together.
- Focus on a dance-like, energetic and lively character.
- Discuss how long the pauses should be; explore different lengths.
- Perform the whole piece to relatives and friends and/or make a recording.

* For suitable sight-reading pieces try *Improve Your Sight-reading!* Grade 1.

Student's worksheet

The Lincolnshire Poacher ingredients

Key signature F major
Time signature $\frac{6}{8}$
Rhythms Ties ♩ ♪
Dynamics *f mf p* <

Articulation Short and slightly accented, *legato*
Character Bold and cheerful
Form Verse and chorus

Terms and signs Boldly, *rit*, *a tempo*, suddenly slower, suddenly faster, ⌒, ♩ = c.104, ♩ = c.69, ♩ = c.126
Special ingredients Chords, tempo changes, stretching a seventh, chromatic fragment

☐ Explore these ingredients by making up little musical patterns, exercises or phrases. Mix and match them where you can. Tick each ingredient when you've used it.

☐ Write out a one-octave F major scale in the right hand, descending in crotchets. Include a clef and key signature. Circle the notes of the triad.

☐ Sight-read this piece and list the ingredients here:

Confidently

☐ Write out bars 17–18 of the left hand, including the correct accidentals with no key signature:

☐ Write out any right-hand two-bar phrase that occurs more than once:

☐ Listen to some other English folk tunes and list them here:

Das Schaukelpferd (Gurlitt)

All about... musical picture-painting, rocking motion, a warm *legato* and clean phrasing

Pre-notation activities

Rhythm

- Choose and clap a suitable pulse in ⁶⁄₈.
- Introduce the upbeat through some simple call-and-response activities.
- Play call-and-response clapping games using two-bar phrases with upbeats, such as:

and longer phrases:

Aural

- Listen to a performance of *Das Schaukelpferd*.
- Clap the pulse as you listen to the performance. Are there any changes of tempo?

Key and scale patterns

- Play the scales and broken chords of C major and A minor in each hand from memory and from notation.
- Play the scale or part of the scale using this rhythm on each note:

Dynamics

- Play a C major scale and broken chord:
  - *mf* and *f*
  - with a *crescendo* ascending and *diminuendo* descending.

Special ingredients

- Make up some broken-chord melodies in ⁶⁄₈ for both hands in C major using *staccato* upbeats, accents, *tenuto* chords and slurred groups of notes.
- Play call and response using short phrases in ⁶⁄₈ and all these articulations.

Title, character and context

- Find out about rocking horses (and the connection with jousting) and improvise little rocking-horse melodies.
- Research whether any other composers have written music about horses or rocking horses.

Introducing the notation (opening the book)

Rhythm

- Look for any recurring rhythmic patterns.
- Clap these patterns from the notation until secure. Continue until able to tap both hands separately and then (section by section) hands together.
- In particular, practise tapping the upbeat and bars 8–9 hands together. Using words to fit the rhythm here may help.
- Discuss and explore ties. How many are there in the piece?

Pulse

- Set up a $\frac{6}{8}$ pulse. Play two bars (hands separately or together), then count and hear the next two bars internally, then play the next two bars and so on.
- Clap along with other pieces in $\frac{6}{8}$, emphasising the two-in-a-bar feel.

Dynamics

- Circle all the dynamics using different colours for the different levels.
- Play bars 1–2 and 3–4 with ⸺⸺ ⸺⸺ (this will help with the phrasing).
- Look at the shape of the dynamics of the piece. What is the difference between bars 1–8 and 15–22?

Aural

- Is this piece major or minor? Discuss the dynamics.
- Play a phrase from the piece twice. The second time make a change for the student to identify.

Key and scale patterns*

- Find patterns in the piece that are based on the scales and broken chords of C major and A minor.
- Explore dominant sevenths (bar 3). Make up a short tune using the notes of the dominant seventh.

Title, character and context

- Discuss the title.
- Think of some words to describe the character of the piece.
- Discuss how the melody in bars 1–2 conveys the rocking-horse image.
- Find out some facts about Gurlitt and listen to other piano pieces by him.

* For more help with scales and broken chords, try the C major Finger Fitness section in *Improve your scales!* Grade 1.

Playing and refining the piece

Rhythm and pulse

- Make up a new right-hand tune to fit over the left-hand chords in bars 1–8.
- Sing or listen to the melody, rocking backwards and forwards in time with it.
- Explore playing the piece at different speeds, including a one-in-a-bar feel.

Key and scale patterns

- Play the scales and broken chords of C major and A minor in a rocking-horse style.
- Discuss the connection between these keys.
- Sight-read a piece in C major.*

Aural

- Regularly try to hear the piece internally – just the rhythm at first, then the melody too.
- Visualise your hands at the keyboard playing the piece at the same time as hearing it internally.
- Listen to, then discuss the articulation and changes of tempo in *Das Schaukelpferd*.

Articulation and dynamics

- Play sections concentrating on the articulation and the dynamics to give the piece its phrasing, shape and character.
- Play the piece with completely different dynamics or articulation, then play it again as written. How different does it sound?
- Make up an exercise to practise the broken-chord patterns (bars 1, 3, 5, etc).

Title, character and context

- Think about the character – does the piece suggest a picture or story or mood?
- What do you think is happening in the *poco rit* bars in the middle of the piece?
- The key feature of this piece is the portrayal of repeated movement. Make sure this is brought to life vividly when performed.

Performing

- Start performing the piece all the way through, hands separately as well as together.
- Focus on a joyful, lively character.
- Discuss and experiment with how much the *poco rit* bars should slow down.
- Perform the whole piece to relatives and friends and/or make a recording.

* For suitable sight-reading pieces try *Improve Your Sight-reading!* Grade 1.

Student's worksheet

Das Schaukelpferd ingredients

Key signature C major

Other scale patterns A minor

Time signature $\frac{6}{8}$

Rhythms

Dynamics *f mf*
decresc,

Character Rocking, cheerful, lively

Form Ternary

Terms and signs
Vivace, poco rit, a tempo, ♩ = c.100

Special ingredients
Stretching a 7th, *staccato* upbeats, accents, *tenuto* chords, ties

☐ Explore these ingredients by making up little musical patterns, exercises or phrases. Mix and match them where you can. Tick each ingredient when you've used it.

☐ Write out both hands of the first four bars of the piece, complete with all terms and signs.

☐ How many bars in the piece contain only notes from the C major triad? _____

☐ Sight-read this piece and list the ingredients here:

Allegro

☐ Make up your own two-bar answering rhythm to these two bars:

☐ Write a poem about or draw a picture of the rocking horse in this piece.

Løvet faller (Nystedt)

All about... gentle shapes, well-balanced hands and a beautiful final cadence

Pre-notation activities

Rhythm

- Choose and clap a suitable pulse in $\frac{3}{4}$.
- One person claps beat 1 and another claps a slightly weaker 2 and 3 – then swap around.
- Play call-and-response clapping games using two-bar phrases:

Aural

- Listen to a performance of *Løvet faller*. Notice the dynamics and the contrast between the slurred and *staccato* playing.
- Clap the pulse as you listen to the performance, emphasising the strong beat of the bar.

Dynamics

- Play an A minor scale and broken chord:
  - *pp*, *p* and *mf*
  - with a *crescendo* ascending and *diminuendo* descending.
- Play an A flat (see bar 10) with a rich, *mf* tone. Then improvise some gentle music incorporating this interesting note.

Key and scale patterns

- Play the scale and broken chord of A minor in each hand from memory and from notation.
- Play the scale (or part of the scale) using this rhythm (and others) on each note:

Title, character and context

- Find out about any famous composers from Norway and listen to some of their music.
- Make up a flowing melody that alternates between the hands.

Articulation

- Make up some patterns in A minor that contrast slurs and *staccato* notes.
- Improvise some gentle music in A minor and $\frac{3}{4}$ based on the two-bar phrasing patterns from the piece.

Introducing the notation (opening the book)

Rhythm

- Look for any recurring rhythmic patterns.
- Clap these patterns from the notation until secure. Continue until it is possible to tap both hands separately and then (section by section) hands together.

Pulse

- Set up a $\frac{3}{4}$ pulse. Play two bars (hands separately or together), then count and hear the next two bars internally, then play the next two bars and so on.
- Clap along with other pieces in $\frac{3}{4}$, emphasising first beat in each bar.

Aural

- Describe the minor-key feel of the piece and the dynamics.
- Sing back some two-bar phrases from the piece.

Dynamics

- Explore the various dynamic levels given in the music and notice how they fit the phrases.
- Apply these dynamic levels to scale and broken-chord patterns in the piece.
- Look for where you might add more detail (such as a *cresc.* and *dim.* in bars 1–4).
- Explore the last two chords: how softly can they be played?

Key and scale patterns*

- Identify patterns in the piece that are based on the scale and broken chord of A minor.
- Identify and discuss the accidentals.
- Explore the left-hand part, making sure the hand position changes are smooth.
- Explore the chords in the final two bars. Practise holding one note whilst moving another note, making sure both hands are exactly together.

Title, character and context

- Discuss the title.
- Think of some words to describe the character of this piece.
- Discuss how the phrase shapes could suggest falling leaves.

* For more help with scales and broken chords, try the A minor Finger Fitness section in *Improve your scales!* Grade 1.

Playing and refining the piece

Rhythm and pulse

- Explore playing the piece at different speeds a little above and below the suggested tempo. Consider which sounds best.
- Tap both lines at the same time whilst tapping the pulse with your foot.

Key and scale patterns

- Play the scales and broken chords of A minor and C major in a gentle, *legato* style.
- Discuss the connection between these keys.
- Sight-read a piece in A minor.*

Aural

- Regularly try to hear the piece internally – just the rhythm at first, then the melody too.
- Visualise your hands at the keyboard playing the piece at the same time as hearing it internally.
- Listen to other *legato* and *staccato* pieces and identify the different articulation.

Articulation and dynamics

- Play the whole piece *staccato* and at varying dynamic levels. What happens to the character?
- Play sections concentrating on smooth phrasing and the dynamics to give the piece its shape and character.
- Explore balance between the hands – give each prominence at the appropriate time.

Title, character and context

- Think about the character – does it suggest a picture or mood? Can you imagine other images apart from falling leaves?
- Discuss how to capture the idea of falling leaves in the sound.

Performing

- Start performing the piece all the way through, hands separately as well as together.
- Focus on a gentle, *legato* character with clear phrase beginnings and endings.
- Perform the whole piece to relatives and friends and/or make a recording.

* For suitable sight-reading pieces try *Improve Your Sight-reading!* Grade 1.

Student's worksheet

Løvet faller ingredients

Key signature A minor
Time signature ¾
Rhythms

Dynamics *pp p mf* — *dim.*
Articulation Mostly *legato*; some *staccato* notes
Character Dreamy, floating, gentle

Form Binary
Terms and signs
Andante ♩ = c.104

☐ Explore these ingredients by making up little musical patterns, exercises or phrases. Mix and match them where you can. Tick each ingredient when you've used it.

☐ Write out both hands of the first four bars of the piece, including all terms and signs.

- Circle the fifth degree of the scale each time it appears in the music above.
- What is the name of the highest left-hand note? _____
- Play the music from your own notation.

☐ Write a two-bar answering rhythm to this:

☐ Sight-read this piece and list the ingredients here:

Gently

mp

☐ Write a poem about or draw a picture of falling leaves.

El cant dels ocells (Trad. Catalan)

All about... creating a mood, a really flowing *legato* and stillness at the end

Pre-notation activities

Rhythm

- Choose and clap a suitable pulse in $\frac{4}{4}$ with a slightly stronger clap on the first beat.
- Explore ♩. ♪ and make up some patterns using this rhythm.
- Discuss the upbeat and play some call-and-response clapping games using:

and similar rhythms from the piece.

Aural

- Listen to a performance of *El cant dels ocells*.
- Clap the pulse as you listen to the performance. Are there any pauses and changes of tempo?

Key and scale patterns

- Play the scale and broken chord of A minor in each hand from memory and from notation.
- Play the scale or part of the scale using this rhythm on each note:

Dynamics

- Play an A minor scale and broken chord:
  - *pp*, *mp*, *mf*, *f*
  - with a *crescendo* ascending and *diminuendo* descending.
- Play call-and-response games using short phrases from the piece, focusing on the dynamic levels.

Title, character and context

- Listen to the version of *El cant dels ocells* by Joan Baez or Casals online.
- Find Catalonia on a map of Europe. Can you find the names of some famous musicians who came from Catalonia?

Special ingredients

- Discuss the word *cantabile* and make up some music in this singing style.
- Improvise some music where the left hand crosses over the right hand.
- Practise broken chords using the pedal.

Introducing the notation (opening the book)

Rhythm

- Look for any recurring rhythmic patterns.
- Clap these patterns from the notation until secure. Continue until it is possible to tap both hands separately and then (section by section) hands together.

Pulse

- Set up a $\frac{4}{4}$ pulse. Play two bars (hands separately or together), then count and hear the next two bars internally, then play the next two bars and so on.
- Clap along with other pieces in $\frac{4}{4}$, emphasising first beat in each bar.
- Discuss pauses and how long the pauses in the piece might be held for.

Terms and dynamics

- Explore the various dynamic levels and notice how they fit the phrases. Look at these in the music. Where is the climax of the piece?
- Apply the dynamic levels to scale and broken-chord patterns and patterns from the piece.
- Make sure all the Italian terms in the piece are understood by making up little improvisations based on them.

Aural

- Discuss why this piece sounds minor. What happens at the very end?
- Sing back some two-bar phrases from the piece.

Key and scale patterns*

- Play a *cantabile*, *legato* scale of A minor and play the broken chord with pedal.
- Identify and play patterns in the piece that are based on the scale and triad of A minor.
- Identify and discuss the accidentals. What is special about the last chord?
- Explore the left-hand thirds (bars 12–16), making sure the notes sound together.

Title, character and context

- Discuss the title.
- Find some other Christmas carols in a minor key.
- Find the English words to this carol.

* For more help with scales and broken chords, try the A minor Finger Fitness section in *Improve your scales!* Grade 1.

Playing and refining the piece

Rhythm and pulse

- Explore playing the piece at different speeds but maintaining the unhurried character and flow.
- Explore the *rit.* and pause in bars 6–7 and think about what happens to the pulse.
- Tap both lines at the same time as tapping the pulse with your foot.

Scales and broken chords

- Play the scales and broken chords of A minor and C major in an unhurried, *cantabile* style.
- Discuss the connection between these keys.
- Sight-read a piece in A minor.*

Aural

- Regularly try to hear the piece internally – just the rhythm at first, then the melody too.
- Visualise your hands at the keyboard playing the piece at the same time as hearing it internally.
- Play each phrase then immediately sing it back.
- Describe the articulation and dynamics in the piece.

Articulation and dynamics

- Play sections concentrating on creating a beautiful *legato*, such as the melody that moves between the hands in bars 1–2.
- Concentrate on adding all the dynamics and details to give the piece its phrasing, shape and character.

Title, character and context

- Does this piece tell a story? Think of some words to describe the character of this music.
- Make up your own 'Song of the birds' or try to write your own words for this piece.

Performing

- Start performing the piece all the way through, hands separately as well as together.
- Focus on an unhurried, *cantabile* character.
- Experiment with how long the pauses and *rits* might be.
- Perform the whole piece to relatives and friends and/or make a recording you can share.

* For suitable sight-reading pieces try *Improve Your Sight-reading!* Grade 1.

Student's worksheet

El cant dels ocells ingredients

Key signature A minor
  (and A major)

Time signature $\frac{4}{4}$

Rhythms ♩ | ♩ ♩. ♪♪ ♩ | ♩.
  ♫ ♩

Dynamics *pp mp f* ⟨ ⟩

Articulation Slurred phrases, pedalling

Character Expressive, gentle, song-like

Special ingredient pedal

Form Improvisatory

Terms and signs Unhurried, expressive, *cantabile*, ⌢, *a tempo, dim. a niente, rit, lunga*, ♩ = c.96

☐ Explore these ingredients by making up little musical patterns, exercises or phrases. Mix and match them where you can. Tick each ingredient when you've used it.

☐ Write out the last three bars of the piece, complete with all signs and terms:

- Name the highest right-hand note _____
- Circle any notes which aren't in the A minor broken chord.

☐ Write down the meaning of each of these:

- *Cantabile* _____
- *Rit.* _____
- *A tempo* _____
- *Dim. a niente* _____
- *Lunga* _____

☐ On which degree of the scale does *El cant dels ocells* start? _____

☐ Sight-read this piece and list the ingredients here:

Expressively

mf

1

The Giant's Coming (Clarke)

All about... story-telling, massive contrasts and energetic triplets

Pre-notation activities

Rhythm

- Discuss what changing metres means, then choose and clap a pulse that moves between 3, 4 and 5 beats in a bar.
- Explore triplets. Play some call-and-response rhythm games using triplet patterns from the piece.

Aural

- Listen to a performance of *The Giant's Coming*.
- Clap the pulse as you listen to the performance. How many pauses are there?
- Describe the dynamics in this performance and the effects they help to create.

Key and scale patterns

- This piece has a tonal centre of A minor. Play the scale and broken chord with a sinister character.
- Play the scale (or part of the scale) using this rhythm on each note:

Dynamics

- Play an A minor scale and broken chord:
  - *pp*, *mp*, *ff* and explore other dynamics
  - with a long, gradual *crescendo* from *pp* to *ff*.
- Play call-and-response games using short phrases and contrasted dynamics from the piece.

Articulation

- Make up some patterns in A minor using:
  - *Staccato* chords
  - Accented notes
  - Accented *staccato* chords

Title, character and context

- Watch a cartoon and listen carefully to the music. Think about how it fits the images.
- Listen to some film music and select your favourite. How does it add character to the film?
- Make up your own short story and write some music to fit it.

Introducing the notation (opening the book)

Rhythm

- Look for any recurring rhythmic patterns in the piece, such as:

and

- Clap these patterns from the notation until secure. Begin by tapping hands separately and then (section by section) tap both lines together.

- Try the piece as a clapping duet, one person clapping each hand.

Phrases

- The phrases are either two- or three-bar patterns: bars 1–3, 4–6, then a series of two-bar phrases and finally a three-bar phrase. Mark these in the music, looking out for the upbeats. Improvise some phrases of similar lengths.

Articulation

- Decide on how to articulate the first (and other) triplets, then explore the various articulations in the music.

- Practise the articulation of bars 7–11, with the *legato* left hand and *staccato* right hand.

Dynamics

- Apply the dynamics to scale and broken-chord patterns and patterns from the piece.

- Explore the short *crescendo* and *diminuendo* shapes (such as bars 3 and 6) and the extended *crescendo* in bars 9–12.

Title, character and context

- This is like film or cartoon music. Make up your own short story or cartoon to fit the piece.

- Compose a piece about giants.

Key and scale patterns

- Identify the chromatic patterns and explore these, looking carefully at the fingering. Make connections with other ingredients such as articulation and dynamics.

Playing and refining the piece

Rhythm and pulse

- Explore playing the piece at different speeds but keeping the sinister, creepy feel.
- Check that the whole piece can be played securely at one clear tempo, especially through the changes of time signature and combinations of triplets and quavers.
- Consider how to count the pause bar (15).

Scales and keyboard geography

- Keep practising the fingering for the chromatic scale patterns by playing hands separately.
- Try starting at different points in the piece.
- Practise the big changes of hand position (bars 6–7, 8–9, 10–11 and 14) to make sure they are absolutely secure.
- Make up a piece that jumps around the keyboard.

Articulation and dynamics

- Play sections concentrating on the articulation and dynamics (especially the *cresc.* and *dim.* and the beginning of phrases) to give the piece its phrasing, shape and character.
- Make sure there is maximum contrast in the dynamics. Experiment with playing some very loud and some very soft notes.

Aural

- Regularly try to hear the piece internally – just the rhythm at first, then the melody too.
- Visualise your hands at the keyboard playing the piece at the same time as hearing it internally.
- Describe the articulation and dynamics in the piece.

Performing

- Start performing the piece all the way through, hands separately as well as together.
- Make sure the keyboard geography of the piece is secure to enable a really creepy, exciting performance.
- Perform the whole piece to relatives and friends and/or make a recording you can share.

Student's worksheet

The Giant's Coming ingredients

Key signature Loosely A minor with much chromaticism

Time signatures 3/4 4/4 5/4

Rhythms

Dynamics *pp mp ff*

Character Sinister, creepy, sad

Form Narrative

Special ingredients Range of keyboard, accurate jumps, slurs, *staccato* and accents

Terms and signs Creepy, Sadly, ⌢ , ♩ = c.92

☐ Explore these ingredients by making up little musical patterns, exercises or phrases. Mix and match them where you can. Tick each ingredient when you've used it.

☐ Write out both hands of the first two bars of the piece (including the upbeat) with all the accidentals and markings. Put a bracket over any chromatic passages.

- Write the names under the left-hand notes.
- Play the music from your own notation.

☐ Write out all the rests which appear in *The Giant's Coming* and a note of the same time value alongside each:

☐ Write out the highest and lowest notes of the piece and give the letter name alongside each:

☐ Draw a cartoon of the giant in this piece.

Calypso Joe (Duro)

All about... repeats that differ, relaxed syncopations and music that makes you smile

Pre-notation activities

Rhythm and pulse

- Choose and clap a suitable pulse in $\frac{4}{4}$.
- Discuss syncopation and play call-and-response clapping games using two-bar phrases such as:

and longer phrases such as:

Dynamics and articulation

- Play an F major scale and broken chord *mf* and *f*.
- Play call-and-response games using short phrases and the articulation from the the piece.

Key and scale patterns

- Play the scale and broken chord of F major in both hands, from memory and from notation.
- Play the scale (or part of the scale) using rhythms from the piece on each note, such as:

Special ingredients

- Discuss sequences and make up some sequential patterns. If possible use rhythms from *Calypso Joe*.

Aural

- Listen to a performance of *Calypso Joe*. Describe the articulation.
- Clap the pulse as you listen to the performance, emphasising the strong beat of the bar.

Title, character and context

- Find out about calypsos.
- Listen to some steel-pan music.
- Find out about how a calypso is danced.

Introducing the notation (opening the book)

Rhythm

- Look for and study the ties. Clap these rhythms with and without the ties.
- Identify any recurring rhythmic patterns.
- Clap the rhythms section by section from the notation until secure.
- Try the piece as a clapping duet, one person clapping each hand.
- Make up some words to help with the tricky rhythms.
- One person claps quavers while the other claps the rhythm of the first two bars, then swap around.

Pulse

- Set up a $\frac{4}{4}$ pulse. Play two bars (hands separately or together), then count and hear the next two bars internally, then play the next two bars and so on.
- Clap along with other calypsos in $\frac{4}{4}$, emphasising first beat in each bar.

Dynamics

- Notice how the two dynamic levels in this simple, binary-form piece fit the phrases. Choose a two-bar phrase and play it at one dynamic, then repeat it at another contrasted level.
- Look for where more dynamics could be added: are there any opportunities for adding *crescendo* and *diminuendo*?

Aural

- Discuss whether the piece is major or minor and listen to the dynamics.
- Sing back some two-bar phrases from the piece.

Key and scale patterns*

- Play the scale and broken chord of F major using a calypso rhythm from the piece.
- Find patterns in the piece based on the scale and broken chord of F major.
- Find the G minor triad patterns in the piece.

Title, character and context

- Explore the calypso rhythm on an electronic keyboard if possible and make up tunes to play along with it.
- Think of some words to describe the character of this piece.
- Try to learn another calypso.

* For more help with scales and broken chords, try the F major Finger Fitness section in *Improve your scales!* Grade 1.

Playing and refining the piece

Rhythm and pulse

- Explore playing the piece at varying speeds and consider which suits a calypso best.
- Tap the rhythm of both lines at the same time and include dynamics.
- Sight-read some pieces with simple syncopation.

Key and scale patterns

- Play the scale and broken chord of F major, C major and D minor in a calypso style. If possible add an accompaniment using Latin American percussion instruments.
- Discuss the connection between these three keys.
- Sight-read a piece in F major.*

Aural

- Regularly try to hear the piece internally – just the rhythm at first, then the melody too.
- Visualise your hands at the keyboard playing the piece at the same time as hearing it internally.
- Sing back two-bar phrases from the piece.
- Clap along and dance to other calypsos.

Articulation and dynamics

- Play sections concentrating on the particular articulations and the dynamics to give the piece its phrasing, shape and character.
- Notice that the final beat of every other bar is *staccato*. Make up a calypso using this articulation.

Title, character and context

- Think about the character of this piece – does it suggest a particular story or mood?

Performing

- Start performing the piece all the way through, hands separately as well as together.
- Do play the piece with the repeats to understand the correct structure.
- Perform the whole piece to relatives and friends and/or make a recording you can share.

* For suitable sight-reading pieces try *Improve Your Sight-reading!* Grade 1.

Student's worksheet

Calypso Joe ingredients

Key signature F major

Other scale patterns
  G minor triad

Time signature 4/4

Rhythms Syncopation

Dynamics *mf* and *f*

Articulation Lightly separated, slurs, single *staccato* notes

Character Cheerful, humorous, jazzy, dancing

Form Binary

Terms and signs Moderately ♩ = c.132 1st & 2nd time bar, Calypso

☐ Explore these ingredients by making up little musical patterns, exercises or phrases. Mix and match them where you can. Tick each ingredient when you've used it.

☐ Write out right-hand bars 9–12 of *Calypso Joe*, exactly as it is written:

- Put a bracket over any broken-chord patterns and name the key: _____
- How many tied rhythms are in the piece? _____
- Give the letter name of the highest note: _____

☐ Add the correct sharps or flats and clef to this scale to make it F major. Circle the notes of the triad.

☐ Write an answering two-bar rhythm to this rhythm from the piece:

☐ Sight-read this and list the ingredients here:

Playfully

mf

p

5

Na krmítku (Eben)

All about... sound colours, crisp *staccato* and an unexpectedly peaceful ending

Pre-notation activities

Rhythm

- Choose and clap a suitable pulse in $\frac{4}{4}$.
- Play call-and-response clapping games using rhythms from the piece:

Aural

- Listen to a performance of *Na krmítku*.
- Clap the pulse as you listen to the performance, emphasising the strong beat of the bar.
- Describe the articulation and changing dynamics in this piece.

Key and scale patterns

- Play the scale and broken chord of C major in both hands from memory and from notation.
- Play the scale (or part of the scale) using rhythms (and articulation) from the piece on each note. For example:

Dynamics

- Play a C major one-octave scale and broken chord:
  - *pp, p , mp, mf*
  - with a *crescendo* ascending and *diminuendo* descending.
- Explore short and extended *crescendos* between one and three bars in length, using scale and broken-chord patterns.

Title, character and context

- Improvise music that focuses on the G to C sharp interval. Discuss the term the 'devil's interval'.
- Play a G harmonic minor scale, looking particularly at the E flat to F sharp interval.
- Listen to some bird song (real or online) and to other pieces about birds.

Articulation

- Make up some patterns in C major using:
  - *staccato*
  - accented *staccato*
  - slurs
  - *tenuto*

Introducing the notation (opening the book)

Rhythm

- How many times does the bar 1 right-hand rhythm pattern return? Find other recurring patterns.
- Clap the rhythm section by section from the notation until secure.
- Try the piece as a clapping duet, with one person clapping the left hand and the other the right. Then swap.

Pulse

- Set up a **C** pulse. Play two bars (hands separately or together), then count and hear the next two bars internally, then play the next two bars and so on.
- Clap along with other pieces in **C**, emphasising the first beat in each bar.
- Find out what the **C** actually means.

Technique

- Work on the left- and right-hand parts separately in bars 8–9; play them with different dotted rhythms.
- Discuss the different articulations included in the piece (*staccato*, accented *staccato*, slurs and *tenuto*).
- Explore and practise all the left-hand chords. Make up a piece using some of these chords.

Dynamics

- Explore and describe the dynamics in this piece. Is there a lot of detail?
- Examine how the dynamics fit the phrases.
- Apply the different dynamic levels to scale and broken-chord patterns and patterns from the piece.

Key and scale patterns

- Identify the accidentals in this piece and see which recur.
- Look for any scale or broken-chord patterns – including those from other keys.

Special ingredients

- Discuss the title.
- Talk about dissonance and consonance. Discuss and explore the dissonant sounds in this piece.
- Explore and compare bars 1–2 with bars 10–11.
- Make up a 'woodpecker' piece using light, crisp *staccato* notes in the right hand and long sustained notes in the left.

Playing and refining the piece

Rhythm and pulse

- Experiment with playing the piece at different speeds and consider whether it is better faster or slower.
- Try tapping the right-hand rhythm with the left hand, and the left-hand rhythm with the right.

Scale and broken chord

- This piece ends in C major and is generally based around the key of C. Play a C major scale and broken chord using as many different ingredients from the piece as possible.

Aural

- Regularly try to hear the piece internally – just the rhythm at first, then the melody too.
- Visualise your hands at the keyboard playing the piece at the same time as hearing it internally.
- Discuss the articulation and dynamics of the piece.

Articulation and dynamics

- Play scales with different articulations from the piece: *staccato*, accented *staccato*, *tenuto* and *legato*.
- Make a recording and listen back to see how clearly defined the different articulations and dynamics really are.

Performing

- Start performing the piece all the way through, hands separately as well as together.
- Focus on the agitated and energetic character of the music and consider which ingredients help to bring this out.
- Perform the whole piece to relatives and friends and/or make a recording.

Student's worksheet

Na krmítku ingredients

Key signature C major
   (with notes from C minor)

Other scale patterns
   G minor

Time signature $\frac{4}{4}$

Dynamics *pp p mp mf*
   $\longleftarrow$ $\longrightarrow$ *cresc.*

Rhythms

Character Mysterious,
   pecking, agitated

Special ingredients
   Accidentals, *staccato*, accented
   staccato, *tenuto*, part playing
   (bars 15–16)

Form Ternary-like

Terms and signs *Poco agitato*,
   ♩ = c.112

and rests

☐ Explore these ingredients by making up little musical patterns, exercises or phrases.
   Mix and match them where you can. Tick each ingredient when you've used it.

☐ Write out bars 6–7 of the piece, both hands, including all the markings:

- Add a bracket over (or under) any semitones.
- Circle the fifth degree of the scale in the right hand.
- Play the music from your own notation.

☐ Write down the meaning of these words and signs:

Poco agitato _____   ♩ _____

Cresc. _____   ♩ _____

pp _____

☐ How many times does this rhythm [rhythm] appear in the piece? _____

☐ Sight-read this and list the ingredients here:

Waddling like a duck

Summary

Pre-notation activities

Key and scale patterns

- Get to know the key, scale and broken chord from memory and from notation and explore related keys too.
- Use call-and-response and question-and-answer activities (playing/ singing).
- Play the scale and broken chord with the various dynamic levels and the articulation of the music.
- Play the scale and broken chord in the character/style of the music.

Rhythm and pulse

- Clap a pulse in the tempo of the music.
- Explore any new rhythms or those particular to the piece.
- Connect these rhythms with the scale and broken chord.

Character

- Listen to and identify relevant musical features in the music.
- Explore other ingredients or concepts found in the music (such as sequences, ostinato, ornaments, intervals and so on).
- Discuss the title.

Introducing the notation

- Look for recurring patterns. How many times do they appear? Are they always the same or do they vary?
- Look for passages based on scale and broken-chord patterns.
- Discuss the key, scale and triad.
- Make sure all the markings are understood.

Further activities for exploration

- Play the scale and broken chord in the style of the music.
- Discuss and explore related keys.
- Tap the pulse with a foot (or use a metronome) and tap the rhythm of the piece or song.
- Improvise using different combinations of ingredients.
- Hear passages of the music internally and then sing them.
- Continually connect with short sight-reading pieces that explore similar ingredients.
- Explore the style and composer (through project work that has been researched on the internet or at a library).

Playing and refining the piece

- Regularly hear the piece internally, particularly thinking about a well-controlled and musically shaped performance.

- Develop images, stories, colours or shapes – any imaginative ideas to help give character to the music.

- Regularly play the scale and broken chord and related keys in the style of the piece.

- Compose a little piece using the structure, style and some of the ingredients from the piece.

- Choose a bar or passage and play or sing it at a different pitch (i.e. starting on a different note).

- Make more connections with short sight-reading pieces that include similar ingredients.

- Practise playing through the piece fluently, understanding and interpreting all the markings.

- Perform the piece to family and friends.

Playing the piece with increasing fluency

- Play sections and/or the whole piece at a variety of speeds.

- Play sections and/or the whole piece with a range of dynamics (beyond those marked in the piece).

- Play sections and/or the whole piece with a variety of articulations.

- Hold the notes down with one hand and play the written notation with other.

- Pupil and teacher play alternate phrases.

Preparing to perform the piece

- Listen to other performances of the piece.

- Record a performance and listen critically.

Use the activities in the following boxes if students need extra work on particular areas.

Scales

Pick and choose from these activities as appropriate

- Identify the key-notes on the keyboard (right and left hands).
- Find the hand position for the first few notes (right and left hands).
- Play the key-note (either hand), hear the first few notes internally and sing those notes. Play the notes.
- Think about the fingering and play a full one-octave version of the scale, broken chord or arpeggio. Then play hands together and more octaves if appropriate.
- Play the pattern upside down! (Descending and then ascending.)

Aural

Pick and choose from these activities as appropriate

- Choose a bar (just one hand or hands together) and hear that bar in your head.
- Play the first note of a scale, broken chord or arpeggio and hear the whole pattern in your head.
- Play a bar (one hand at a time), hear it in your head, and then sing it.
- Play the same bar again and then sing it, changing one note.
- Find a short piano piece online with similar ingredients, listen to it and then describe its features: smooth or detached notes; loud or soft; major or minor; does it change speed?

Pulse and rhythm

Pick and choose from these activities as appropriate

- Clap the pulse of the piece at an appropriate tempo.
- Clap the first beat of the bar and hear the other beats in your head.
- Tap the pulse and with a foot and clap the rhythm of the right and then the left hand.
- Tap the pulse and hear the rhythm of each hand in your head.
- Are there any repeated rhythmic patterns in the piece?
- Tap the rhythm of the left and right hands together.

Reading

Pick and choose from these activities as appropriate

- Choose a bar, set a pulse going, play the first note, try to hear that bar in your head and then play it.
- Play a bar a few times, play it from memory and then write the bar down from memory. Check it is correct!
- Read as much of the piece as possible in your head (in other words, hearing the music internally.)

Improvisation

Pick and choose from these activities as appropriate

- Make up a short piece using just the key-note, but any rhythms from the piece.
- Make up a short piece based on the scale of the music.
- Choose two or three ingredients from the music and make up your own piece.
- Make up your own short piece based on the same title.
- Make up an exercise to practise a tricky bit.

Timeline

Grade 1 composers

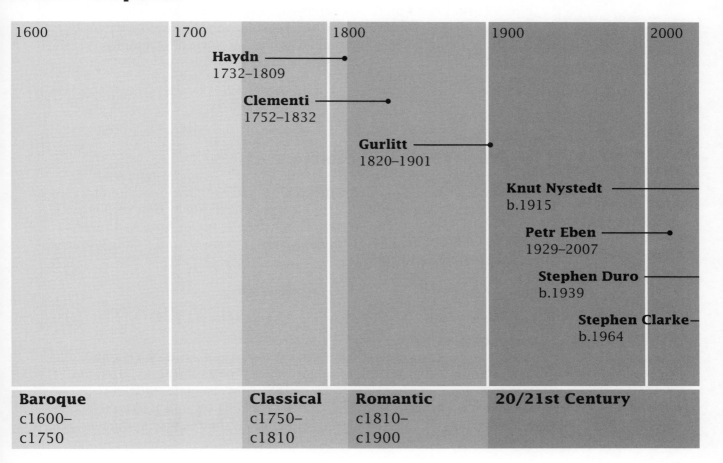

1600	1700	1800	1900	2000

Haydn
1732–1809

Clementi
1752–1832

Gurlitt
1820–1901

Knut Nystedt
b.1915

Petr Eben
1929–2007

Stephen Duro
b.1939

Stephen Clarke
b.1964

Baroque
c1600–
c1750

Classical
c1750–
c1810

Romantic
c1810–
c1900

20/21st Century

Also by Paul Harris

Improve your aural!

Designed to take the fear out of aural through fun listening activities, boxes to fill in and practice exercises, these workbooks, each with CD, focus on all the elements of the aural test. A range of interconnected activities are included to help develop the ear, including singing, clapping, playing your instrument, writing music down, improvising and composing. Fulfils all ABRSM exam requirements.

Improve your sight-reading!

This series of workbooks is designed to help overcome sight-reading problems, especially in the context of graded examinations. Step by step players build up a complete picture of each piece, first through rhythmic and melodic exercises, then by the study of prepared pieces with associated questions for the student to answer, and finally with a series of practice tests.

Improve your scales!

Using 'finger fitness' exercises, scale and arpeggio study pieces and simple improvisations, Paul Harris' brilliant method teaches students to know the notes and thus to play scales and arpeggios with real confidence. Forms a solid basis for the learning of repertoire and sight-reading techniques, as well as being invaluable preparation for exams.

Improve your theory!

Covering all the requirements for ABRSM theory exams, these workbooks are firmly rooted in Harris's highly successful *Simultaneous Learning* approach. Learning theory has never been so much fun or seemed so natural! Seamlessly linking theory to pupils' own pieces and utilising aural and compositional skills, these books will transform how theory is learnt and improve every aspect of musicianship.

To buy Faber Music publications or to find out about the full range of titles available please contact your local music retailer or Faber Music sales enquiries:

Faber Music Ltd, Burnt Mill, Elizabeth Way, Harlow CM20 2HX
Tel: +44 (0) 1279 82 89 82   Fax: +44 (0) 1279 82 89 83
sales@fabermusic.com   fabermusicstore.com